Look Look!
There's Our God

THIS BOOK BELONGS TO:

____

Look Look! There's Our God

Shelley Dedrick
Sierra Brown

XP BOOKS

XP BOOKS
2301 Lucien Way #415
Maitland, FL 32751
407.339.4217
www.xulonpress.com

Printed in the United States of America.

LCCN: 2019-908400

ISBN-13: 978-1-54567-222-8

To my grandchildren, whom I love with all my heart.
My prayer for you is that through God's word
and His magnificent creation, you will experience His love,
come to know him, love Him, and follow His ways.
You matter.
Love, Mimi

Dylan and Hadley were playful and curious little children. Their minds were filled with lots of great questions.

The children had been learning about God, but sometimes they were confused. Why? Because they could not actually see their God. They could see their swings, their toys, and their food, but seeing God—well, that was a bit harder.

"I wish He was easier to see!" they said to their mother.

When springtime arrived, Hadley and Dylan went on a hike with their mother. The grass was growing greener, the trees were filled with blossoms, and colorful wildflowers smelled so good.

"We can't see Him. Where is our God?" they asked as they walked.

Suddenly, they saw a giant field full of wildflowers on the trail. "Look, look!" Said Momma. "See the bright colors? Smell the sweet flowers?"

With eyes full of wonder, they said "Yes, yes, yes, we can! There's our God. Let's go pick some flowers for Mimi!"

And they did.

One summer day as they played in the park, they said to their mother, "We can't see God, Momma. Where is He?"

Momma smiled at them and said, "Look, look! There He is. See the tree branches swaying? Feel the wind on your face?"

Their eyes grew larger
and they said,
"Yes, yes, yes, we can!
There's our God. Let's go fly a kite!"

And they did.

While the children were playing, it started to rain.
Walking to the car, they said, “We can’t see God. Where is He now?”

Momma stopped and pointed at the sky. “Look, look.” she said.
“There He is. See the rain falling? Feel the raindrops on your face?”

Their eyes twinkled and they said, "Yes, yes, yes, we can!
There's our God! Let's go splash in a puddle."
And they did.

Autumn came. The air was getting colder and the trees were turning red, yellow and orange.

"We can't see God, Momma. Where is He?"

"Look, Look," said Momma. See the colorful leaves falling to the ground? Hear them crunch under your feet?

"Yes, yes, yes, we can!" said Dylan and Hadley.
"There's our God. Let's go jump in the leaves!"
And they did.

Soon it was Thanksgiving Day, and Dylan and Hadley were driving to their Mimi and Pop Pop's for turkey dinner.

"We can't see Him, Momma," they said, "Where is he?"

A big smile filled Momma's face as she pointed out the car window.

"Look, look, see those big strong mountains?"

With excited voices they answered,
"Yes, yes, yes, we can! There's our God.
Let's go tell Mimi and Pop Pop about Him!"
And they did.

One morning Dylan and Hadley awoke to a big surprise. It snowed while they were sleeping! After breakfast, they bundled up and went outside to play in the snow with Momma.

"We can't see Him. Where is He?"

Momma laughed and said, "Look, Look. See the white snowflakes falling from the sky?"

"Yes, yes, yes, we can!" said the children. "There's our God. Let's build a snowman!"

And they did.

At bedtime, Dylan and Hadley were once again full of questions. "We can't see God when it's dark, Momma. Where is He?"

Their mother pointed out the window. "Look, look. There He is. See the stars in the sky? See the moon shining bright?"

They shouted together,
"Yes, yes, yes, we can! There's our God!
Let's count the stars."

And they did.

Just before Momma tucked them in, she knelt down on the floor. Holding them close in her arms, she said, "Would you like to know one of God's best and most special creations?"

Dylan and Hadley's eyes opened wide. "Yes! What is it?"

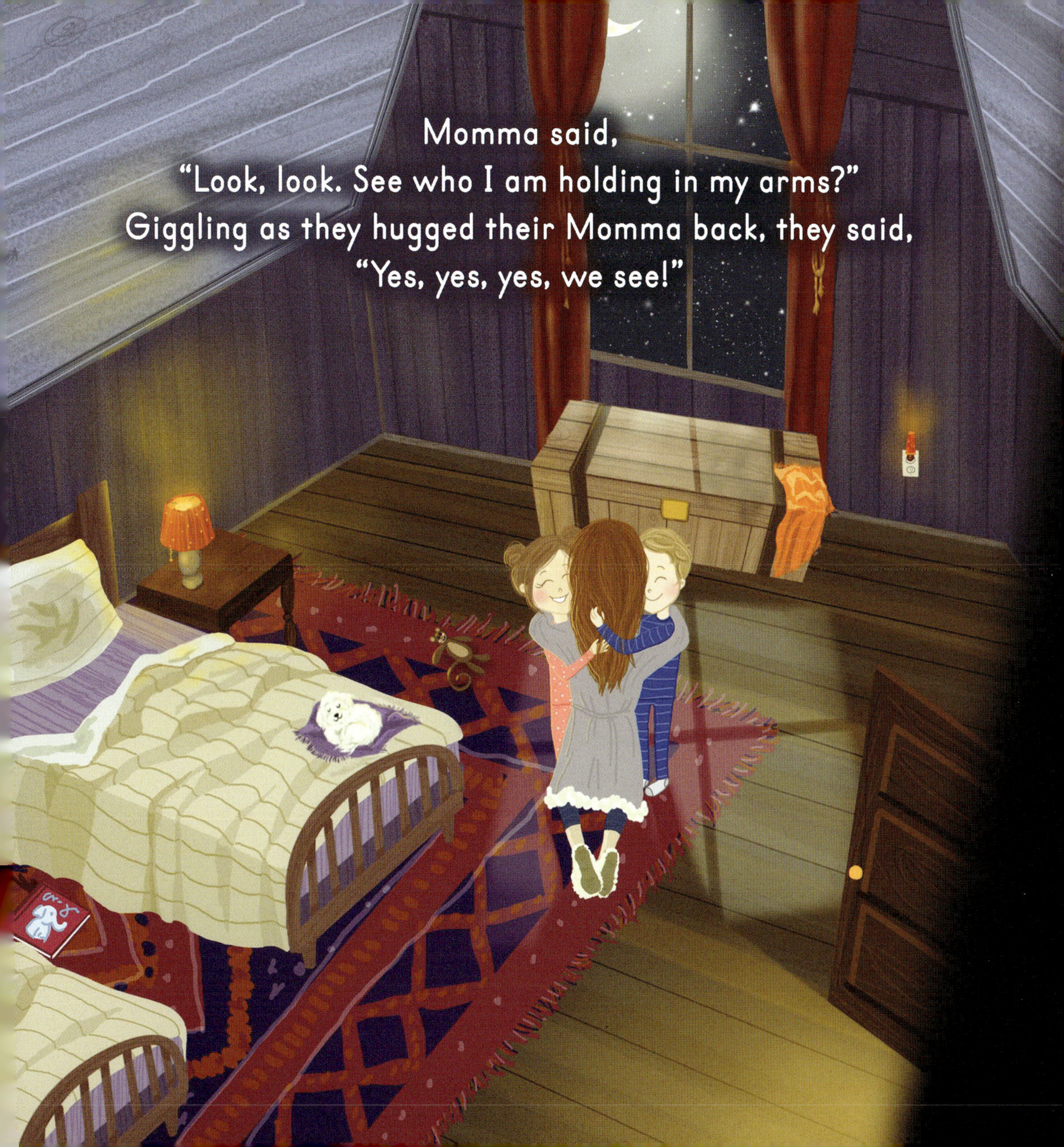
Momma said,
"Look, look. See who I am holding in my arms?"
Giggling as they hugged their Momma back, they said,
"Yes, yes, yes, we see!"

As the days passed, Hadley and Dylan learned that they could find God all by themselves, any time and anywhere.

Most importantly though, God could be found in people. All you have to do is "Look, look!"

And they did.

Romans 1:20
For since the creation of the world God's invisible qualities -
his eternal power and divine nature -have been clearly seen,
being understood from what has been made,
so that men are without excuse.

THE HEAVENS DECLARE THE
GLORY OF GOD
THE SKIES PROCLAIM THE
WORK OF HIS HANDS.
day after day THEY
POUR FORTH SPEECH;
night after night THEY
REVEAL KNOWLEDGE.
THEY HAVE NO SPEECH, THEY
USE NO WORDS; NO SOUND
IS HEARD FROM THEM. Yet
THEIR VOICE GOES OUT INTO
all the earth,
THEIR WORDS TO THE ENDS OF
THE WORLD. Psalm 19:1-4